Obi Onyefulu was born in Onitsha, Nigeria.
He studied for several years in the United States,
and took a doctorate in Modern European History
at Florida State University. Since his return to Nigeria,
he has lectured at Anambra State College of Education,
and published a number of textbooks on Nigerian history.
He is an avid collector of Nigerian folk tales.

Evie Safarewicz trained as a ceramic designer before becoming
a freelance illustrator. She is an enthusiastic traveller, taking a particular
interest in the peoples and landscapes of Africa. Her previous books
include *Steaming Cook Book* (Collins), *Bouquet de Provence* (Pavilion),
A Proper Breakfast (Johnson Editions), *Grandma's Garden* (Dorling Kindersley)
and *The King Who Wanted to Touch the Moon* (Ginn & Co.).
Evie's other title for Frances Lincoln is *The Warrior and the Moon*
by Nick Would, which explores the spirit and beliefs of the Maasai.

To my mother Emily Nkemjika, my sisters Ifeoma and
Chinye, and to my daughter Emily Nkiruka – O.O.

Chinye copyright © Frances Lincoln Limited 1994
Text copyright © Obi Onyefulu 1994
Illustrations copyright © Evie Safarewicz 1994

First published in Great Britain in 1994 by
Frances Lincoln Children's Books, 4 Torriano Mews,
Torriano Avenue, London NW5 2RZ
www.franceslincoln.com

Distributed in the USA by Publishers Group West

This paperback edition first published in Great Britain and the USA in 2007

British Library Cataloguing in Publication Data available on request

ISBN 978-1-84507-178-3

Illustrated with watercolour and pencil

Set in Palatino

Printed in China

CHINYE

A WEST AFRICAN FOLK TALE

RETOLD BY OBI ONYEFULU
ILLUSTRATED BY EVIE SAFAREWICZ

F

FRANCES LINCOLN
CHILDREN'S BOOKS

Long ago there lived a girl called Chinye. Her mother and father were dead, so she lived with her stepmother Nkechi and her stepsister Adanma.

Every day Nkechi made Chinye do all the work and sent her back and forth through the forest to fetch water. Chinye was a quiet, obedient girl, and she worked as hard as she could to please Nkechi. She got no help from Adanma, who was spoilt and lazy.

One night, there was no water in the house to cook
supper. Adanma had used all of it for a bath. But it was
no good trying to explain this to Nkechi.

"Go to the stream at once and get more water, you
bad girl," she shouted angrily.

To reach the stream, Chinye had to go through
the forest. Wild animals prowled there, and even on
moonlit nights the bravest villagers stayed at home.
Chinye begged Nkechi to let her borrow water from
a neighbour instead. It was no good.

"Be off with you!" Nkechi shouted, thrusting
the heavy waterpot into Chinye's arms.

Weeping, Chinye set off into the forest. Danger lurked behind every tree. A lion roared, and her heart jumped.

Then, right in front of her, a shape loomed up on the path. Chinye screamed. Too terrified to run, she shut her eyes and prayed.

"Where are you going, child?" asked a gentle voice. Chinye opened her eyes in wonder. By the light of the moon, the shape looked like an antelope.

"To the stream, to fetch water," she whispered.

"The forest is no place for you at this time of night," the voice said. "Go home."

Chinye shook her head. "I can't. My life is bad enough already, without making my stepmother angry!"

The shape sighed and let Chinye pass.

A little further on, a second shape appeared. This one looked like a hyena. Once again Chinye screamed and shut her eyes, but the creature's voice was full of love and kindness. Hearing why Chinye was out so late, it said: "Go on your way with my blessing. But take care – a lion is following me. Hide behind this tree and wait until it has passed."

When the lion had gone, Chinye crept out from behind the tree and hurried on towards the stream. She hastily filled her waterpot, then ran back the way she had come.

Suddenly, right in front of her she saw an old woman, bent with age.

"Bless you, child," she told Chinye, reaching out as if to hold her. "Listen to me. As you go on your way, you will pass a hut, and hear the sound of drums and singing. Go in, and you will find the floor of the hut covered with gourds – some big, some small, some quiet, some noisy. One of them will call to you, 'Take me!' but do not take it: it is full of evil things. Choose the smallest, quietest gourd and when you get home, break it open on the ground."

The old woman blessed her again, and disappeared.

Sure enough, in a little while Chinye heard
the sound of drums and singing, and there
by the path, in the moonlight, stood a hut
she had never seen before. Chinye lowered
her waterpot carefully to the ground and went in.

Everything was just as the old woman had said.
Gourds of every shape and size covered the floor,
and from one of them a voice cried "Take me!"
but Chinye remembered the old woman's warning.
She searched until she found the smallest,
quietest gourd and took that instead.

Once more the figure of the old woman appeared.
  "You have chosen wisely," she said. "Make good
use of whatever fortune brings you." She stretched out
a hand and touched Chinye tenderly on the cheek.
"Now, go home in peace, my child."

Nkechi was waiting at the door of their hut.

"What took you so long?" she demanded, glaring. "And what's that in your hand?" She pointed suspiciously at the gourd Chinye was carrying. "An old woman gave it to you? What's inside?"

She snatched the gourd and rattled it violently, but it made no sound and she tossed it aside.

"Hurry up and build a fire. We've waited long enough for food tonight," she shouted.

So there was no chance for Chinye to break open the gourd that night.

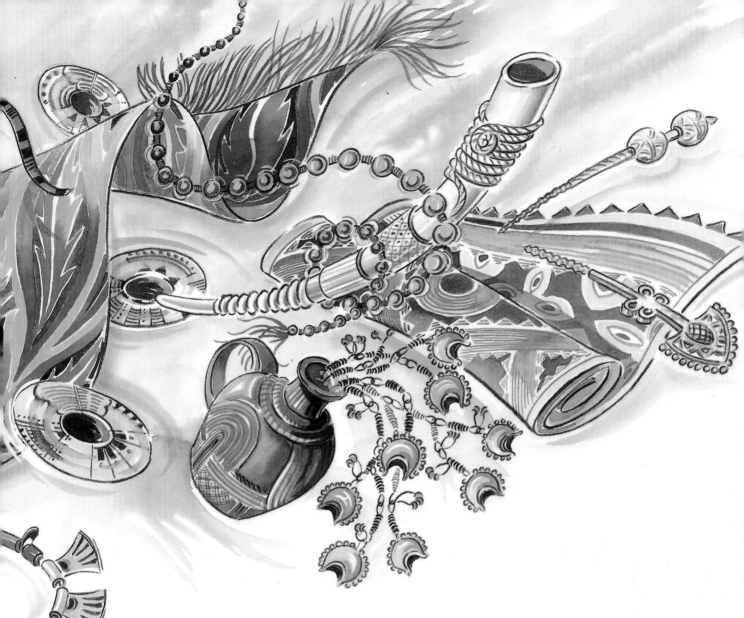

Next morning, Chinye awoke early. Nkechi and Adanma were fast asleep. Chinye found the gourd and crept out to her father's hut, then locked the door and smashed the gourd on the ground.

At a stroke the bare hut was transformed into a treasure-house: gold ornaments spilled across the floor, mingled with ivory and swathes of rare damask in all the colours under the sun. Chinye rubbed her eyes. Then she ran to wake her stepmother.

When Nkechi saw the treasure, for once in her life she
was speechless. To think that such treasure had come
from a gourd! Why couldn't it have been Adanma
who met the old woman?

Aha! Nkechi's eyes gleamed greedily. Maybe it was
not too late!

That very night Nkechi carried out her plan, and sent
Adanma down to the stream to fill the pot. Like Chinye,
Adanma met the antelope, the hyena and the old woman.
But unlike Chinye, she paid no attention to the old
woman's advice, and when she came to the hut and heard
one of the biggest gourds say "Take me!" she did just that.

"Look, Mother," she said proudly when she got home. "I chose the biggest gourd I could!"

Nkechi rubbed her hands: the bigger the gourd, the greater the treasure. And with a cry of "We're rich! We're rich!" she snatched the gourd from Adanma and dashed it to the floor.

There was a flash of light and a clap of thunder. Nkechi and Adanma screamed and clutched each other. A great whirlwind sprang up, gathered up all their belongings and flung them out through the window – pots, pans, clothes and cowrie shells were swept away into the night. Nkechi and Adanma had lost everything.

Too proud to ask Chinye for help, Nkechi left the village for ever, taking Adanma with her.

And Chinye? She used her wealth to help the people of her village and lived happily ever after.

MORE PICTURE BOOKS IN PAPERBACK
FROM FRANCES LINCOLN

THE COMING OF NIGHT
James Riordan
Illustrated by Jenny Stow

When the great river goddess Yemoya sends her daughter Aje
to marry a chief in the Land of Shining Day, Aje pines for the dark
shadows of her mother's realm. So her husband sends Crocodile
and Hippopotamus down to the river to bring back a sackful of Night …
A Yoruba creation myth from West Africa that will delight young readers.

Suitable for National Curriculum English – Reading, Key Stages 1 and 2
Scottish Guidelines English Language – Reading, Levels B and C

ISBN 0-7112-1378-X

THE TIME OF THE LION
Caroline Pitcher
Illustrated by Jackie Morris

At night-time, when Joseph hears a Lion's roar, he decides, against
his father's advice, to go and meet the Lion. He sleeps beside him,
meets his brave lioness and watches the cubs play, learning
that danger is not always where you think. Then one day,
traders come looking for lion cubs...

Suitable for National Curriculum English – Reading, Key Stages 1 and 2
Scottish Guidelines English Language – Reading, Level C

ISBN 0-7112-1338-0

THE LEOPARD'S DRUM
Jessica Souhami

Osebo the leopard has a fine, huge, magnificent drum,
but he won't let anyone else play it – not even Nyame, the Sky-God.
So Nyame offers a big reward to the animal who will bring him the drum...
How a very small tortoise outwits the boastful leopard is dramatically
retold in this traditional tale from West Africa.

Suitable for National Curriculum English – Reading, Key Stage 1
Scottish Guidelines, English Language – Reading, Level B

ISBN 0-7112-0907-3

Frances Lincoln titles are available from all good bookshops.